EDGING

SENSUAL POEMS

APAR SINGH

Made with ❤ on the Notion Press Platform
www.notionpress.com

This collection of poems is dedicated to the energy that I feel. The energy that liberated me, and continues to give new wings to my imagination.

Helplessly and hopelessly,

Love you each moment of day.

Heartlessly and ruthlessly,

Each time you push me away.

It's the energy due to which art exists in this world, and every artist craves for. Like my previous ones, this work too is dedicated to the same heavenly energy.

I desire only one thing girl,

Priceless, impregnable heart.

Feelings cannott get any real,

Don't stop now, let me start.

Contents

Contents

Foreword

Apar

Eyes and ears girl,

Are senses from far.

Tongue, nose, skin,

Are desires of Apar.

Ember

Your lips feel like embers,

Can't stop touching them.

Tonight as desire thunders,

Won't try controlling them.

Depths

Say what you keep hidden,

In the depths of that heart.

Listen to what's forbidden,

For bodies won't stay apart.

Preface

There are times when we realize that what we really want. The only question is when and how we realize it. Every one goes through the same phases, emotions and experiences, only difference is when and how.

A man who can't get the women he needs, is either the luckiest or un-luckiest. Which which are you?

Truth behind every man's anger,

Is a woman who fucks another guy.

How could be at his best temper?

Sadly there are things money buy.

Prologue

Bosoms

Shelter me in your bosoms,

Comfort me in your scent.

I've been looking for peace,

For once you could relent. Why?

Woman

Never got the love of a woman,

Did I lonce ive after being born?

Never could suck pointed nipples,

Did it alone, never a pussy torn.

Lover

I am not a perfect lover,

And a very imperfect man.

Today, tomorrow, and ever,

Love you like back then.

Long-s

1. Bird Box

A sexual tension simmers,
And I could even explode.
A shag need to give myself,
And I must relive of my load.
I wish to go all the way in,
And you I must push back.
As I am go on my way out,
Why then you pull me back?
Let the dust settle down girl,
Before I lift your hidden lid.
You are so wet down there,
My footlong will simply skid.
I have seen your bird box,
Accept my folly, my mistake.
If I could melt you before,
You'd know the hiding place.

2. Boring

Do you mind if I bore you?
Can't stop self from asking.
Everyday I shall bore you.
You'll find it to your liking.
Inviting is your fine waist,
I gaze at your sexy navel.
Right now I wanna taste,
Your sari wanna unravel.
Wanna bite your rosy lips,
Your killer waist-ass ratio.
Throat you down to the ribs.
Kneel on you at the patio.
I wanna press your bosom,
Feel your pointed nipples.
As you grab a long demon,
Bunt hands down, ripples.
Insert in wide, open mouth,
Overflow it with my spout.
Shotgun your two oranges,
A head-butt, and you shout.
If you understand feelings,
And care for my thoughts.
I'll be patient, of kneelings,
Reciprocate, beating hearts.

3. Kiss

I wanna hold your body,
For there's no finer lady.
Night saw me in hubby,
A girl that is so so shady.
I hear your voice and,
Feel like touching myself.
Why not ever show me,
How you do it yourself.
I desire the pull your lips,
Bite thighs, caress your hips.
Untie hair, pull those clips,
Need you to touch at all tips.
I wanna wrench your wrists,
Thrust deeper into your hole.
Suck those pointed nipples,
Biting all your hidden moles.
I wanna grab heavenly ass,
Tighten my grip on yours.
Pin you down and lift up,
Drill you down like hoars.
Give you a pain tip to tip,
And fulfil unsaid desires.
Kissing your fragile lip,
Dousing those unlit fires.

4. Mole

There's a mole in a hole,
Badly wish it was mine.
Can I brush her thighs?
Send shiver up the spine.
There's a pole in a dole,
Dream her cave always.
That's mysterious of all,
Take her front, sideways.
There's a wood in a hand,
Need her's to be relaxed.
Rat the pussies all-times,
Should've already asked.
There is a irksome cock,
Hard as a mountain rock.
Why not slide your hand?
And be ready for a shock.
Look at crazy sturdy dick,
Lately been acting a prick.
Runs thru her gams slick?
And give her life's real kick.

5. Up/downside

Her hair enjoys fingie,
She knows my thingy,
Feet never miss point,
Screw my bling-blingy!
Tipsy smile fuels me,
Shine in eyes kills me.
Pull her erotic lingerie,
A hand-ful, no quickie.
It's time to not refrain,
Feels go down in drain.
Tear apart your dresses,
Only I'll make it a train.
We're all things nooky,
She could sit atop me.
Back-sides are finicky,
Press cute butts, belly.
Slowly whisper in ears,
Pet, churn her knockers.
Hot and heavy in years,
Long pleasures, in tears.
Crazy is my condition,
Still not lying be-side.
Will bore it deep, fatal,
Both upside, downside.

6. Bored

Bored her out by opening fists,
Look at with my long to-do list.
Openly told desires of a heist,
Instead of stealing a secret kiss.
To bore her did want to in a way,
The way a man in love wants to.
Lost way, no play, pushed away,
Hope she knows, and wants too.
A burning fire bores me inside,
Keep me in a never ending high.
Search a women's body to hide,
Only lust, like her can none find.

7. Beg

I want to hear you beg,
For me to start and stop.
Wish to hear you scream,
And listen to your moans.
I wanna hear your whispers,
Explore your intimate parts.
My endless wait to undress,
Use chocolates, vanilla bars.
I want you to hold my heat,
And feel passions in my veins.
I want you to jump and slide,
If you want, can take the reins.
I wanna touch, kiss and caress,
De-flower you between the legs.
Push all of me inside that dress,
Tongue, and sip down to dregs.
It is roller coaster ride darling,
Desire of some passionate sex.
If you do not want me kissing,
Then could you kiss me instead?

8. Juicy

Your kohl rimmed eyes,
And shiny ruby red lips.
Can you tightly grip it?
Slowly rub it on my tips.
Your face shines in flair,
As fingers I run thru hair.
Smooching a long tongue,
Before biting a lovely ear.
Kills your gentle smile,
Each & every single time.
Bite your yummy neck,
Rubbing shoulder to spine.
Your slim, fragile arms,
Long and sleek thighs.
Need to give it strokes,
Taking you to new highs.
Your juicy melon bosoms,
Badly need my uncovering.
Your tight butts, high heels,
Pluck you, and de-flowering.
Grazing your bare back,
How do I think straight?
In love we're already late,
Hope endlessly isn't wait.

9. Wanna-be

I wanna be your wonder,
And wanna be your awe.
I wanna be your pleasure,
It's you I wanna make thaw.

I wanna be your excitement,
And I wanna be your safety.
I wanna be your powerhouse,
It's with you wanna see nasty.

I wanna be your predicament,
And I wanna be your intensity.
I wanna be your lawlessness,
It's you I wanna drink honestly.

I wanna take you too slow,
And I wanna be a little hasty.
I wanna make us moan, blow,
It's time I wanna take off 'T'.

10. Frequency

Ahead of science,
I'm a fucking art.
I'm the frequency,
No ending, no start.
I have everything,
But always broke.
This time I bring ,
Hope in one stroke.

Short-s

11. Big

Big
Not many have taken,
My big one inside them.
Desire for bed broken,
She'll always deny them?
Before-After
Will make you eat chocolate,
I keep an ultra thin rubber.
Will eat up your wet pussy,
I keep ice bursts to up her.
Matter
Only you matter to me,
And you must know why.
Could anytime use me,
With you only ain't shy.

12. Cum

Cum
You know what I need,
Where do I come from.
You don't know real me,
Taste where I cum from.
See
I see that table besides you,
All want is to lay you on that.
I see that window behind you,
Desire of pushing against that.
Life
She has a certain life,
Lives a certain lifestyle.
She is someone's life,
Loves this boy freestyle.

13. Digging

Digging
I cannot stop digging,
There's no better base.
I've damaged the hole,
Turn to your pretty face.
They
They've got it all wrong!
Women take who they want,
And men take who they can.
If needs, one can - else can't.
Else
Yes she was loved by me,
Like nobody else has been.
Yes she was sucked by me,
Like nobody else has been.

14. Front-Back

Front-Back

Wish she slept at front seat,

I would have parted her lips.

After taking her to back seat,

I would have pressed till ribs.

More

Can I come inside you?

My heart aches for more.

Can I snap back at you?

My hunch says for sure.

Ask

This time won't ask you,

Only gently touch you there.

Missed my chances a few,

Give a kiss you know where.

15. Hard

Hard

I need to listen hard,
Plan it hard to the d.
I need to do it hard,
Push it hard to the d.

Toil

As mind toils endless,
Body needs now hers.
Blood boils so helpless,
Tounge melts into hers.

Beg

Do not make me beg,
I need font of your milk.
Trust me I am in a bag,
I need body made of silk.

16. Head

Head

Oh, I love head massage,

Maybe you can give me one.

To heart a direct passage,

Relax me, leave me undone.

D-ripping

A few drops dripping,

She's taken it off now.

I've taken a whipping,

To bed her somehow.

Li-cked

I licked her salty orange,

Cut it with sharp wood.

Ate her in such manner,

Never before felt so good.

17. Loose

Loose

Can you take a day out with me?

And make me lose in tug of war.

Can sneak out one night with me?

Will make you loose in tub of war.

Embrace

We will embrace tight girl,

To make each other whole.

Lubricate each other at 69,

Penetration, hole and pole.

Hot-el

She won't sent me a selfie,

Just posted a pic this morn.

No touch up, keeps a scent,

No earing, no dress adorn.

18. Milk

Milk
Why have to leave tonight?
Stay, let's milk one another.
Like warriors we must fight,
Until we're finished together.
Squeeze
She can say 'Squeeze Me',
For I don't mind doing that.
Better even says 'Feel me',
Hard ground, rough on a mat.
Neck
Place hands on your neck,
Want to tell you my desires.
Will make up for all pent up,
Let me touch, douse all fires.

19. Pen-etration

Pen-etration

To increase penetration,
I will have to but diversify.
Lower the concentration,
For so many must satisfy.

Weak

She went weak in knees,
As I walked towards her.
She was wetting panties,
I left with one next to her.

Sy-energy

The energy I oft flushed,
Could have come handy.
If in synergy she trusted,
Could've been her candy.

20. Power Play

Power Play

Raring to win over, go all out,

Must show her my power play.

Memories of the hooks & pulls,

Until next time, she will replay.

Luck

How come I found you?

I can't believe my luck.

The feels are everything,

Forever could give a fuck.

Deflower

Many have de-flowered her,

Re-flower each time I must do.

Transient have un-covered her,

Will un-layer her without ado.

21. Spoon

Spoon
If I'm little or big spoon,
It does not really matter.
Anyways if it's with you,
Whether before or after.
Now
You're now abreast to me,
As we melt into one another.
Could whisper 'Now' to me,
Feel, stop thinking together.
Take me
Take me for just once girl,
Even if you don't love me.
Suck lollipop in trance girl,
In passion, don't judge me.

22. Wooden

Wooden

Wooden it be nice?

One night, do it thrice.

Your body cold like ice,

Burn in my fire, vice.

Waited - Why?

I waited for her till eve,

She agreed to come by.

Lights went out for long,

Didn't kiss or touch thigh. Why?

Dress

Puts on dress that rips off,

But I have got no car on me.

I could bang her in my car,

But I have got no Thar on me.

23. Out

Out

Quietly she was dipping,

Opportunity, asked her out.

Now that she's dripping,

Tonight will not pull it out.

Up

When you're my dream,

Why'd I want to wake up?

Desire your sexy scream,

Why'd I want to give up?

Suction

I will change you forever,

Suck lips in such suction.

Can you keep us together?

I shall never malfunction.

24. Water-fall

Water-fall
I will eat up as you read,
Turn you into a waterfall.
Can fulfil your every need,
You're a goddess after all.
Grab
In this unreal world,
Real is only your thigh.
Grab your apple flower,
Real is only your high.
Leash
None can put a leash,
She is such a wild bitch.
Crazy, still is her wish,
Desire with her to hitch.

25. Side

Side

Lucky is the guy who clicks her,
Says, take mine like this a few.
Wish you too say to me one day,
Come, take me from this side too.

Black Panther

Did you see a black panther,
In the deep and dense forest.
Already had enough of banter,
Long, thick one for my hottest.

Both

You're both desire and need,
I could become yours too.
My body and soul you feed,
Can fill some of yours too?

www.ingramcontent.com/pod-product-compliance
Lightning Source LLC
Chambersburg PA
CBHW022124150726
47990CB00003B/1498